SIWITI — *A Whale's Story*

TEXT BY

PHOTOGRAPHY BY

SIWITI — *A Whale's Story*

ALEXANDRA MORTON
ROBIN & ALEXANDRA MORTON

ORCA BOOK PUBLISHERS

Canadian Cataloguing in Publication Data

Morton, Alexandra, 1957–
    Siwiti, a whale's story

ISBN 0-920501-97-4

    1. Killer whales — Juvenile literature.
I. Morton, Robin (Robin A.)   I. Title.
QL737.C432M67 1991   J599.5'3
C91-091111-8

Design by Christine Toller
Printed and bound in Hong Kong

First hardcover printing, 1991

10   9   8   7   6   5

Publication assistance provided by The Canada
Council.

Orca Book Publishers
PO Box 5626, Station B
Victoria, BC Canada
V8R 6S4

Orca Book Publishers
PO Box 468
Custer, WA   USA
98240-0468

To my son Jarret and Siwiti.
Watching them grow strong has filled
my life with joy.

THE eagle emerged from the grey wisps of fog that clung to the mountainsides. As she flew, her sharp eyes scanned the water below. Every movement on the surface drew her attention; nothing escaped her brilliant yellow eyes. Although the eagle wasn't hungry, high in the ancient cedar tree at the head of the bay, her two half-grown eaglets never stopped crying for more food. This was the finest season for hunting. The salmon were now close to their home rivers, and they appeared in huge numbers in the shallow water. The eagle knew she wouldn't have to ride this current of air for long before spotting another bright silver salmon to feed her family. She drifted slowly over the surface of the water.

As the eagle dipped one wing and glided around a steep rocky point, her heart raced with excitement. There were whales in this bay! Though the jet black backs of the killer whales were impossible to see in the dark green water, their brilliant white patches flashed beneath the surface. The eagle swooped lower and made a circle above the bay, hoping to spot a school of salmon corralled among the orcas. She opened her strong beak, and her wispy cry floated out into the mist. Certainly there must be fish here.

But all she could see were the whales. She circled once more and landed on the long outstretched branch of a fir tree. From the stability of her perch she stared intently at the scene below.

Most of the whales were gathered at the mouth of the bay, milling in circles. They spyhopped often, bringing their heads high out of the water and looking into the centre of the cove. The eagle cocked her head and heard the muffled calls of the whales beneath the water. In the middle of the bay, four whales lay close together, barely moving.

For a time the eagle was confused. Where were the salmon? Had the whales eaten every one of them already? She crouched to take off from her perch, when suddenly, one of the whales sped off across the bay. The orca spun as she slashed through the water. Her belly flashed white, then her dorsal fin broke the surface, then her belly showed again. At once the water around the orca darkened. The other whales rushed towards her. And just as suddenly, all four disappeared from view.

The eagle bent to straighten a feather, but an instant later, she stopped and raised her head again. Something had emerged from the dark water in the centre of the bay.

The newborn killer whale thrashed about on the surface, confused and desperately gulping air. The cold water stung, and her tail — with its flukes still folded together like butterfly wings — was almost useless. The only thing familiar to the little whale was sound. While growing inside her mother, she had always been surrounded by the rhythms of the sea and the calls made by her family. Now these sounds, much louder than before, were her comfort. This was where she belonged.

As the baby orca struggled, something firm pressed up against her, supporting her from below. A loud noise vibrated along the length of her body. Siwiti instantly relaxed; it was her mother. A great whoosh of air rose powerfully from the hole on top of Mother's head. Without thinking, Siwiti released a little puff of air as well. For the next forty years, most of the breaths the two whales would take would be together.

Siwiti wriggled gently on her mother's back, and slowly her body took its proper shape. Her floppy little tail spread its wings until it became a stiff and useful paddle. The tiny dorsal fin lifted off her back and soon sat upright like a sail. Within twenty minutes, the newborn whale was ready to travel.

The mother whale sank down, and Siwiti slid into the deep green water. Though she now swam gracefully enough, her tail could only push her straight ahead. She still had to learn to steer. As she tested her new found skills, the water quickly became too shallow. Whoosh — one of the helping whales brushed in front of Siwiti, guiding her away from the sharp, rocky shoreline. Mother swept in alongside her baby, and together they rose to the surface.

When Mother came up to breathe, she rolled smoothly along the surface. But Siwiti wasn't quite sure where the cold water ended and the misty grey air began. So with an extra wiggle of her tail, she shot out of the water, exposing half her body. The other whales could see that the calf was strong. Their calls rang with excitement, alerting the rest of the family. It wasn't often that a whale was born.

When the morning fog lifted, the four females left the bay with their young charge. Siwiti felt the presence of the other members of her family as they pressed around her. Their calls rang out and vibrated along the length of her body. One of the adults nudged Siwiti until she swam just behind her mother's dorsal fin. There the water seemed to suck her in close and cradle her. The exhausted newborn closed her eyes and rode on her mother's current, tucked in between the tail and dorsal fin. Her mother swam slowly with the group. Though she too was worn out from the ordeal of giving birth, she was content to have a baby with her again.

As the moon grew fuller, Siwiti quickly learned to use her streamlined body. She found her pectoral fins and began to steer herself at last. Soon she was streaking alongside her mother as they chased schools of Pink salmon. Siwiti was fascinated by the salmon, although she had no use for them yet. Many times a day she rolled her soft rosy tongue into a funnel and drank her mother's rich warm milk in huge gulps.

Day and night, the whale family travelled through the cold green water. As Siwiti became a better swimmer, she could turn her attention to the fascinating world around her. Most interesting of all was her big brother, who could do everything, and Siwiti found him irresistible. His calls were like the calls of the adults, not like her baby chirps. And Big Brother could swim up to the air above, plunging right out of the water. When he fell back again, he was surrounded by bubbles of light, which swirled about him and hurried back to the surface.

One night, when the pale moonlight made the white patches on each whale shimmer and glow, a quiver of excitement rippled through her family or pod. Everyone began to swim faster. They passed gleaming schools of salmon without bothering to chase them. They entered a swift-flowing passage and were swept along in its current. Mother was making happy noises, not like the ones she made after filling her belly with fish, but higher pitched sounds which felt like questions to Siwiti. The little whale swam with the pod, gracefully slipping in and out of her mother's current. Before long, she became aware of faint calls. She knew the sounds were made by other killer whales, because these calls were similar in some ways to the sounds her own family made. Cautiously, Siwiti tucked in behind her mother again. Big Brother wriggled with anticipation.

The sounds grew louder and louder, until out of the blue-green water of early morning, another pod appeared. There were large whales like Uncle and some the size of Mother; others were like Big Brother. There was even another baby peeking out from behind the dorsal fin of its mother.

Siwiti spent the day gathering her courage to join the other young whales before dashing back to the safety of her mother's side. Siwiti had never seen the games these new whales were playing. For a time, everyone took turns pushing their tails as far as possible straight up out of the water. Wobbling, with their noses pointed downwards, the young whales balanced as long as they could, until at last they fell over. Later they attempted to raise their pectoral fins in the air and slap the water as quickly as possible. Siwiti was entranced. But as the day wore on, the need for a rest overwhelmed the little whale. At last she tucked into her mother's current and closed her eyes.

Siwiti awoke suddenly. Her mother abruptly changed direction and swam straight up through the water. But when she reached the surface, she kept going. For an instant, almost half of Mother's body was out of the water. Siwiti spyhopped alongside her mother. The sun was now low in the sky, and streaks of brilliant colour showed in the west.

Then Mother joined four other females. Together they dove straight down side by side, their tails pumping in unison. Without warning, the divers spread their pectoral fins. Instantly they were streaking for the surface. Siwiti, unable to turn quickly enough, rammed into the whale next to her. The large female slowed for an instant. But once she was satisfied the baby was not hurt, she raced off just behind the other four.

Siwiti gave up the chase and watched the larger whales streaking for the light. When they burst into the air, the four leaders faced the sun, all in a row, their white chins glistening and their pectoral fins straight out in front of them. The fifth orca broke the surface just as the other four slid back.

The sun was very low and the sky had turned orange, but the whales did not stop. Every member of the pod dashed about, chasing, splashing and rolling over each other in a frenzy of activity. Friends, relatives and strangers touched Siwiti gently, and the little whale touched them back. Strangers became friends, and the young whale's bond for her family was now stronger than ever.

As the weeks passed, Siwiti noticed that the air she inhaled deep into her lungs was growing colder. Now when it became dark, the air often tingled sharply against her warm insides. Her family no longer swam with others. In fact, for several days now, only half her family was around her. As always, she swam with Mother and Big Brother. Granny still swam ahead with Uncle. But it was strange not to hear everyone else calling out. Siwiti also noticed that there were no longer any schools of flashing salmon to chase. Instead, Mother ate the prickly fish that lived in the forests of kelp.

At first Siwiti was afraid to venture into the thick mass of kelp. She swam anxiously in circles when her mother disappeared from view. It was one thing to play with a single ribbon, but quite another to swim through the dense forest of waving arms, where she might be trapped and unable to reach the air. But her family's calls were so full of pleasure, the young whale's curiosity soon overcame her fear.

Siwiti rose to the surface three times to change the air in her lungs, making sure the last breath was as big as she could possibly manage. Her eyes were wide with excitement as she plunged into the forest. At first, the ribbons slithered all over her face and she couldn't see. But Big Brother rubbed up beside her, and her heart calmed a little. Soon she relaxed and found that the slippery kelp fronds felt wonderful. There was nothing to fear after all. She was much stronger than the kelp. She raced in and out of the dark green forest.

There was so much to learn.

One calm sunny day, Siwiti was gliding along upside down, watching two seagulls trying to steal a wriggling fish from a third gull. The three birds swooped and twisted through the air, just as three young whales might chase each other through the water. Siwiti was fascinated. How did those birds stay up there? Whenever she tried to leave the water, she splashed back down almost immediately.

As Siwiti swam, a dark form suddenly blocked her view of the gulls. With a quick thrust of her tail, the young whale dove in alarm. But the strange creature didn't follow, and Siwiti resurfaced, now more curious than afraid. She had never seen a deer before. It didn't look like food, and since it definitely did not want to play, Siwiti swam around it several times, then left it alone.

It wasn't long before Siwiti realized that most of the creatures she met were afraid of her. Among the most timid were the fat harbour seals. Sometimes the fearful little creatures bobbed on the surface, remaining as still as possible, waiting for the whale to disappear. Other times, they watched Siwiti from the beach, their huge soft brown eyes following her as she moved past them. Siwiti would have loved to play with the harbour seals, but they didn't seem to want to play with her.

Not everyone was afraid of her, though. Dall porpoises liked to play and chase fish with Siwiti's family, and they were faster than any creature Siwiti had seen before. They flashed by in a blur of black and white or zigzagged in front of Uncle. He enjoyed their company as he pushed them along with the waves created by the movement of his head. Siwiti tried to swim with them, but it wasn't easy to keep up. They could take a breath much more quickly than the little whale. In a burst of spray, they were up, down again and gone.

Late one afternoon, Siwiti and her family passed a large rock surrounded by kelp. There was a strong taste coming from the kelp bed, a taste the young whale had never encountered. Big Brother didn't seem interested in exploring, but Siwiti was curious, so she entered the kelp forest alone. The slippery kelp tickled her in places that only it could reach — the notch in her tail and beneath her pectoral fins.

Siwiti was busily exploring the forest, when suddenly she saw a flash of brown through the dense kelp. Then there was another on her other side. Frightened, she began to swim backwards away from the rock. But Siwiti was still not very good at swimming backwards, and the kelp tangled around her tail, slowing her down. Whoosh Another brown flash of fur shot right past her face and turned. A big round eyeball glared at her. The sea lion opened its mouth and slashed his long teeth at the little whale.

Without warning, they were everywhere. Some were as big as she was, swooping, charging and snapping their big teeth at her. Siwiti was terrified. As she turned to escape, a set of long teeth scratched across her dorsal fin. Siwiti exploded straight up into the air, her breach scattering the sea lions. She raced back to her mother's side. Granny, Big Brother and Uncle nuzzled the little whale as well. Never again would Siwiti allow herself to be surrounded by sea lions.

In winter, Siwiti's pod spent much of their time in the deep, steep-sided inlets. The sounds there were different. Waterfalls crashed straight into the ocean from great heights. Shrimp snapped and crackled like the sound of bacon frying, and rock cod grunted loudly in the kelp beds. And sometimes everything was still and very quiet. In the open water, close sounds blended with distant noise, but in the inlets there were only close sounds.

Once, when Siwiti and Big Brother were taking turns pushing each other to the surface, their mother's sound disappeared. Both young whales suddenly felt the terrifying silence of being alone. Mother noticed immediately that she and Granny had rounded the point and could no longer hear the young ones. Both whales spun around and swam back, making their loudest calls. Relief washed through the youngsters as they raced home to the coziness of Mother and Granny. Even Uncle had returned from the middle of the inlet to make sure everything was all right.

One morning it began to snow. As Siwiti rolled
smoothly on the surface to breathe, the air she inhaled
tickled more sharply than ever before. In surprise she
snapped her blowhole shut and dove. Rolling over, Siwiti
looked into the sky. It was full of flakes, which made
fascinating patterns as they swirled. Siwiti swooped down,
feeling the pressure squeeze her body as she travelled
deeper. Then she spread her pectoral fins and pointed
herself again towards the surface. Five times she pumped
her flukes as hard as she could. With an explosion of
spray, Siwiti broke out into the snowstorm. For an instant,
she twisted her entire body among the flakes. Then, with
a crash, she became a sea creature again.

Later that day, the sun came out and glistened brightly on the snow. The two young whales spent most of their time swimming upside down looking at the strange whiteness. As the adults worked hard to find enough fish to eat, Siwiti wandered along the shoreline, passing beneath the heavy cedar branches, which were so full of snow, they trailed in the water.

A soft unfamiliar sound carried through the water, hee . . . yawww. Siwiti flipped right side up. But before the little whale could investigate, Mother appeared with the rest of the pod. Granny took the lead, and the family turned into the nearest bay. Uncle, Granny and Mother lined up side by side with their heads pointing in one direction. Big Brother and Siwiti could feel the tension in the group. They stayed very close on either side of Mother. The five whales spun slowly like the blades of a propeller. The sounds coming from Granny were unlike anything Siwiti had ever heard. The old whale bellowed out deep vibrating grunts instead of her usual musical calls. All three adults snapped their jaws with a loud clacking noise.

Siwiti became afraid of the soft hee . . . yawwws, even though she had no idea what made them. The green water was too murky for her to see. After the tide had fallen a little lower, Granny led the pod out of the bay. Siwiti pressed in close to Mother and opened her mouth slightly to let the sea water pass over her tongue. The water carried the taste of killer whales. But unlike all the whales she'd met before, there was no scent of fish on the strangers. These whales tasted of sea lions instead.

Siwiti was bewildered. All the other killer whale groups they had encountered were considered friends, but this pod was somehow different. It was clear they would avoid these sea lion-tasting whales with their soft eerie calls.

Some of the bays that Siwiti and her family swam past were full of people, who seemed like most peculiar creatures. But the little whale was more intrigued by people in boats. They came in a wide variety of shapes. Some of them looked like logs and had a little tail they plopped in and out of the water on either side. But most had tails which spun around very rapidly instead of going up and down like tails should.

One of the creatures was a scientist, whose behaviour seemed especially strange to Siwiti. It was obviously friendly. Whenever they passed the bay where it lived, it hurried out buzzing loudly. It was clear that the creature didn't want to be left behind.

One calm winter day, Siwiti spyhopped to check on the scientist. When the young whale had her entire head out of the water, she heard a faint sound come from the creature. It was a bit like one of Siwiti's family calls. She spyhopped again to make sure. The friendly creature was definitely trying to use one of her family's calls. Siwiti was stunned. Even the youngest calves never made the mistake of using a sound that didn't belong to its family.

While the air was coldest and the land mountains were white, there were times when the water rose very high and covered places that were dry the rest of the year. The family explored low cedar branches and thick prickly grasses, which tickled their bellies as they skimmed along. But their visits were always short. Land was one of the few things Granny seemed to fear. When it was time to go, Granny's call had a note of urgency that Siwiti could not ignore, despite her intense curiosity. Giving in to the pull of the deeper water, the little whale would eventually follow her mother away from the shallows and back to the world where they belonged.

As the sun began to spend more time in the sky than the stars, Siwiti was once again caught up in the excitement of the returning salmon. She was still dependant on her mother's milk, so she didn't need to eat them, but nothing compared to the excitement of chasing salmon. As the fish streaked ahead, their bodies flashing silver, the taste of salmon filled Siwiti's head. But it was difficult to keep up with the fish. If they turned too quickly, Siwiti often swam on ahead in confusion, wondering where the fish had disappeared to.

Sometimes the fish hid in the kelp or nosed their way into a crack in a cliff. Once a salmon entered a crack, Mother would put her nose against the rocks and pump her tail up and down with powerful strokes, creating huge waves. Then the fish would be washed out by the water surging through the crack.

At times the salmon was wedged in so tightly, it couldn't be flushed out. Then Mother would give up, her nose creased from the pressure of the rock. Big Brother could push himself in farther; sometimes the creases on his face went almost up to his eyes. Siwiti would get the last chance to flush out the salmon. She was so much smaller than the others that she could squeeze in far enough to stick her tongue out and lick the fish. But she could never get her mouth open enough to bite it. It was always time to go before she could manage to get a grip on the salmon.

Chasing salmon gave Siwiti a chance to practice the most important skill she had to master: the ability to see with sound. When Siwiti was a few months old, she became aware that some of Mother's calls told the family where she was and what she was doing. Other sounds were used to see what was ahead in the dark green water. These sounds were very loud like all of Mother's sounds, but shorter and sharper — painful if they hit the young whale. Siwiti quickly learned to stay beside or behind her mother when these sounds were being used. As she followed along, she could hear every sharp click go out and return. But whenever it came back, the sound was different.

As they chased fish, Mother clicked quickly and continuously while scanning her head from side to side. If some of the clicks bounced back faster than the others, it meant that a fish was close, and Mother would swerve towards it. At first, Siwiti bumped into her mother whenever she swerved, but soon the little whale learned to follow the sound as well. Soon they moved together like one creature.

Siwiti practised making clicks when she was sure no one was in front of her. At first her clicks sounded like a scoop of mud hitting a warm rock: "splut, splat." Siwiti tightened up the muscles inside her blowhole to form the sound, "putt, pitt." If she practised too long, the muscles inside her head would ache, and Siwiti would have to quit for the rest of the day. Eventually, she developed a proper crisp little click: "tink, tink, tink."

Now that she could produce clicking, Siwiti was able to go up to a kelp forest and sound her way through the green ribbons. If anything besides another whale splashed near her in the dark, she could point her little clicks in that direction and find out what it was. She could even look down and discover how deep the water was. Sometimes the little clicks she sent to the bottom got lost and never returned. Then, confused and anxious, the little whale would rush to the comfort of her mother.

One evening, as the family was sleeping down an inlet — side by side, breathing together like one huge whale with many fins — faint calls brought everyone awake. Immediately, Siwiti reached out and touched Mother, remembering the strange whales they had avoided. But as the sound was repeated, Siwiti recognized one of the calls that belonged to Granny's sister. The young whale rubbed against Big Brother in anticipation. She had almost forgotten about this other part of their family.

Uncle pushed ahead, while the rest of the family swam behind him side by side. Uncle seemed very excited. He lunged sideways out of the water and lifted his tail straight up into the air, moving his pectoral fins in order to raise himself even higher.

Siwiti wanted to race ahead, but she resisted; it was better to wait until Uncle calmed down. Listening carefully, she could hear another bull lunging and splashing ahead of the approaching group. The scientist was there as well, sliding back and forth between them. Finally, after a very long time, Siwiti's aunt, great aunt and cousins were visible in the pale green spring water.

Siwiti had never felt anything as wonderful as the warm bodies of her extended family nuzzling her on all sides, after so many months without them. To the little whale, it was the feeling of home after a long absence and warmth after cold bitter winds. Winter was over, and the time of summer gatherings and clouds of silver fish had returned.

Photograph by C. Bennett

Author's note

SIWITI is a real little whale. She was born in 1983 and continues to grow and learn in the green waters of the Pacific Northwest. All the adventures described in this book are based on events I have witnessed over the past eleven years of observing Siwiti's family and the other whales who share this area. Some things are very rare; four whales spyhopping side by side is something I've seen only once, and young whales approaching sea lions is also an unusual sight. But playing with kelp and flushing salmon out of crevices are common events. Siwiti and her family are constantly revealing more of themselves to me. Because of their immense creativity, I know I will never have seen it all. Many of their actions are difficult to understand. Most days when I head my boat for home, I'm filled with more questions than answers.

On the other hand, there is one aspect of their nature that becomes clearer with each encounter: their strong sense of family. A whale's family — or pod — is also her home. Siwiti will never experience the security of a den or take shelter in a cave. She lives at the dynamic interface of air and water. Whether it is glassy calm or blowing hurricane force, she must return to the surface every few minutes. And so her security is the presence of her family around her. Even Big Brother will stay with Mother his entire life, and when she dies, he will most likely remain at Siwiti's side. If Siwiti dies or is captured, Big Brother will wander between groups of relatives, as I have observed with other males who have lost their immediate family. I am very happy to have Siwiti as part of my life. I feel strongly that there must always be a place in this world for her and her kind.

Postscript:

Siwiti is a whale's story. Whales are part of a living system and for some to live, others must die. Siwiti died in 1996. We almost never know how or why a whale dies; they just disappear. But we do know that Siwiti's family tree never divides by choice. So when a member of the family disappears for a year or more, we assume that member is dead. Siwiti's mother Yakat, her aunt Kelsy, and her two sisters and one brother are still thriving however. Though many whales on the west coast of North America are suffering from the toxins we have loosed into the oceans, Siwiti's family lives far enough to the north, away from urban centers, to be minimally affected.

In the ten years since *Siwiti* was first published I have watched some runs of salmon, the life-blood of this coast, decline, while others are now in spectacular recovery. In particular, Siwiti's favorite, the little pink salmon is flourishing. In 2001, these fish defied fishery statistics and poured past my house in unexpected abundance. A river of life. The heavy rainfall that autumn allowed these fish to swim higher into the watersheds to spawn than ever recorded. This species of salmon — perhaps the healthiest protein on earth because they are short-lived and feed low on the food chain — will benefit all life that surrounds them, from birds and bugs to whales and humans. As we continue to learn how to live with our animal neighbors, we will see this bloom of life return all around us.

Alexandra Morton
Echo Bay
December 9, 2001